The Headless Horseman Rides Tonight

MORE POEMS TO TROUBLE YOUR SLEEP

by **JACK PRELUTSKY**

illustrated by **ARNOLD LOBEL**

GREENWILLOW BOOKS, New York

Text copyright © 1980 by Jack Prelutsky
Illustrations copyright © 1980 by Arnold Lobel
All rights reserved. No part of this book may be reproduced, or utilized in any form
or by any means, electronic or mechanical, including photocopying, recording or by
any information storage and retrieval system, without permission in writing from
the Publisher, Greenwillow Books, a Division of William Morrow & Company, Inc.,
105 Madison Avenue, New York, N.Y. 10016
Printed in the United States of America First Edition 1 2 3 4 5 6 7 8 9 10

Library of Congress Cataloging in Publication Data
Prelutsky, Jack.   The Headless Horseman rides tonight.
Summary: Presents 12 scary poems. 1. Children's poetry, American.
[1. American poetry] I. Lobel, Arnold. II. Title. PS3566.R36H4
811'.54 80-10372 ISBN 0-688-80273-7 ISBN 0-688-84273-9 lib. bdg.

For Harry Wilks
whose floor
provokes nightmares

CONTENTS

THE MUMMY

In the darkness of a sepulcher
   beneath the shifting sands,
the mummy stirs within its sheath
of rotten linen bands.
Inside its stone sarcophagus
beneath the pyramid,
it moves its cloth-enshrouded hands
and pushes back the lid.

It arises in that chamber
where no living thing has stepped,
in that chamber chill and airless
where for centuries it has slept,
then it stumbles through the mazes
of the labyrinthine halls,
and with powers supernatural
beats down the earthen walls.

Now it walks the scorching desert
all its being filled with rage,
ancient rage it's borne for eons
since a dim primordial age,
and it staggers blindly onward,
mud-encrusted, caked with clay,
and it permeates the desert
with the stench of foul decay.

Now it must unleash its fury,
spew the venom of its wrath,
and woe to those poor souls who cross
the mummy's mindless path,
for the mummy will destroy them,
they will perish, wracked with pain.
There is terror in the desert
for the mummy walks again.

THE SPECTRE ON THE MOOR

In the ghostly, ghastly silence
of the misty misty moor,
a phosphorescent spectre
sets upon its twilight tour,
searching for some hapless victim—
it will find one, oh be sure.

It swirls about the vapors
of the luminescent mist
with its tendrils slowly writhing,
deadly purpose in each twist,
and its grasp is cold and final,
not a creature can resist.

Do not go there in the twilight,
do not heed its dread allure.
It will hold you and enfold you
in such ways you can't endure,
till you never leave the spectre
on the misty misty moor.

10

THE TOWERING GIANT

In a darksome dominion
remorseless and cold
stands a towering giant
grotesque to behold.
He hulks like a mountain,
his head in the sky,
and all who approach him
will certainly die.

The towering giant
by stretching his hand
turns trees into sawdust
and rocks into sand.
One stamp of his foot
and the mountaintop shakes
and the winds turn to tempests
with each breath he takes.

Should you land in his clutches
he'll grind you to crumbs,
or crush you to powder
beneath his great thumbs.
The towering giant
a thousand feet tall
will reduce you to nothing . . .
to nothing at all.

12

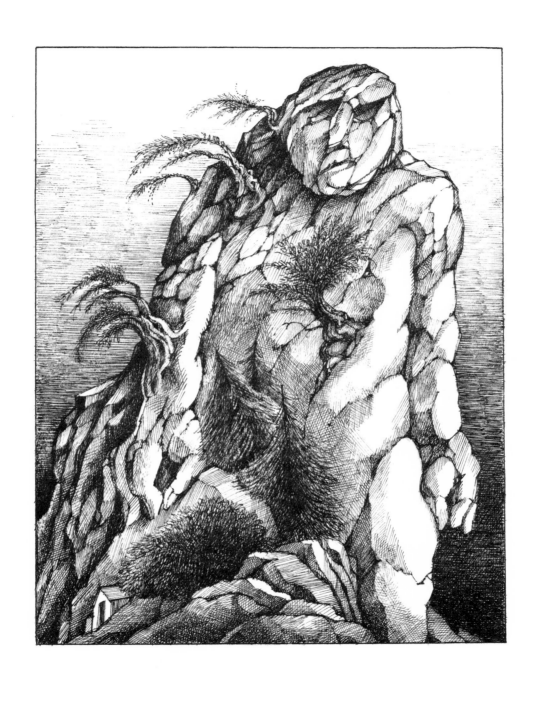

THE ZOMBIE

Upon your bed you sleep in pain
    for nightmares whirl within your brain.
You waken with a fearful start
as horror grips your heart.

You sense a presence standing there,
then all at once it meets your stare.
A zombie waits within your room
and with it dwells your doom.

And you shiver and you scream
and you hope it's all a dream
as the zombie nears your bed.

The zombie, spawn of voodoo's charms,
has come to take you in its arms.
It longs to crush, it yearns to clutch,
and lethal is its touch.

It does not live, yet is not dead,
two sockets burn within its head.
It does not see, it does not hear,
it does not heed your fear.

And you shiver and you scream
and you hope it's all a dream
as the zombie nears your bed.

Closer, closer to your bed,
closer comes this thing undead.
It nears you at a steady pace
and oh! its awful face!

Closer, closer, closer still
the zombie nears with icy will.
Its face remains expressionless
as you feel its cold caress.

And you shiver and you scream
for you know it's not a dream
as the zombie nears your bed.

THE KRAKEN

Deep beneath the foaming billows
   something's suddenly amiss
as a creature wakes from slumber
in the bottomless abyss,
and a panic fills the ocean,
every fish in frenzy flees
for the kraken has awakened
at the bottom of the seas.

It rises to the surface
with an overwhelming noise
and it hunts for mighty vessels
which it crushes and destroys,
then it chokes a great leviathan
with one stupendous squeeze—
oh the kraken has awakened
at the bottom of the seas.

How it lashes, how it thrashes,
how it flashes, how it flails,
how it dwarfs the greatest fishes,
even dwarfs the mighty whales!
Nothing living in the ocean
can enjoy a moment's ease
for the kraken has awakened
at the bottom of the seas.

THE DARKLING ELVES

In wildest woods, on treetop shelves,
  sit evil beings with evil selves—
they are the dreaded darkling elves
and they are always hungry.

In garish garb of capes and hoods,
they wait and watch within their woods
to peel your flesh and steal your goods
for they are always hungry.

Through brightest days and darkest nights
these terrifying tiny sprites
await to strike and take their bites
for they are always hungry.

Watch every leaf of every tree,
for once they pounce you cannot flee—
their teeth are sharp as sharp can be . . .
and they are always hungry.

THE SORCERESS

In flowing dress
  the sorceress
begins her evil toil.
She stirs her vat
of filth and fat
and sees it seethe and boil.

Midst hellish smells
she whispers spells
and does a deadly dance,
with words of death
upon her breath
she slips into a trance.

Higher, higher
burns her fire,
distant is her voice,
and Hades' hole
takes one more soul
as demons there rejoice.

In flowing dress
the sorceress
falls swooning to the floor—
her brew grows cold,
her tale is told,
her victim lives no more.

THE INVISIBLE BEAST

The beast that is invisible
is stalking through the park,
but you cannot see it coming
though it isn't very dark.
Oh you know it's out there somewhere
though just why you cannot tell,
but although you cannot see it
it can see you very well.

You sense its frightful features
and its great ungainly form,
and you wish that you were home now
where it's cozy, safe and warm.
And you know it's coming closer
for you smell its awful smell,
and although you cannot see it
it can see you very well.

Oh your heart is beating faster,
beating louder than a drum,
for you hear its footsteps falling
and your body's frozen numb.
And you cannot scream for terror
and your fear you cannot quell,
for although you cannot see it
it can see you very well.

THE ABOMINABLE SNOWMAN

In the shadows of a mountain
  where the light is ever dim
and the snows are ever blowing,
stalks a visage great and grim.
Through the bone-benumbing wilderness
he travels on alone—
the abominable snowman
is the name by which he's known.

He wanders through the vastness
of the cold and lonely slopes,
and he watches as he wanders,
and he hungers, and he hopes,
and he searches for his quarry—
luckless mortal, small and frail,
in that unrelenting whiteness
where the winds of winter wail.

Those who stray into the compass
of that unforgiving place
vanish from this earth forever,
evermore without a trace.
There are none to see them suffer,
there are none to hear them moan,
as he tears them into pieces
and devours them to the bone.

The abominable snowman
that few eyes have ever seen
trudges homeward through the mountains
where that home has ever been,
homeward to his hidden stronghold
that a mortal may not know.
The abominable snowman
disappears within the snow.

THE BANSHEE

The baleful banshee, pale and worn,
frail and haggard, long forlorn,
wails from midnight until morn,
and her eyes are red with weeping.
She combs her foul and filthy hair
and shrieks into the midnight air,
and oh my child, you'd best beware,
she'll rouse you from your sleeping.

She calls from near the river's side,
and calling, she'll not be denied.
It does no good to run and hide,
it's death she is forecasting.
When she sings out a mortal's name,
that life eternity shall claim—
to substitute for earthly flame
the slumber everlasting.

Upon the night that she appears
to send her song into your ears,
she'll not abide your pleas and tears,
the banshee scorns your sorrow.
So pray she does not come this night
if you would see the morning's light—
sleep well my child, sleep fast and tight,
and dream of sweet tomorrow.

THE POLTERGEIST

Something strange is flitting through your hair,
but when you try to find it, nothing's there.
You know, though, when it gives your cheek a bite,
a poltergeist is in your house tonight.

Your rocking chair is rocking by itself,
and all your books have tumbled from the shelf,
and something keeps on flicking out the light—
a poltergeist is in your house tonight.

The chandelier has shattered on the floor,
and things unseen are rapping on the door,
and when you look, no creature meets your sight—
a poltergeist is in your house tonight.

Within the kitchen cups and saucers shake,
and there before your eyes the windows break,
and when it laughs, you scream with all your might—
a poltergeist is in your house tonight.

THE HEADLESS HORSEMAN

The headless horseman rides tonight
through stark and starless skies.
Shattering the silence
with his otherworldly cries,
he races through the darkness
on his alabaster steed.
The headless horseman rides tonight
wherever the fates would lead.

     And he rides upon the wind tonight,
     he rides upon the wind,
     galloping, galloping, galloping on
     out of the great oblivion,
     galloping till the night is gone,
     he rides upon the wind tonight,
     he rides upon the wind.

The headless horseman rides tonight
begarbed in robes of black
to bear a being from the earth
never to bring him back.
He is evil's foul embodiment,
with laughter on his breath.
The headless horseman rides tonight,
the minister of death.

And he rides upon the wind tonight,
he rides upon the wind,
galloping, galloping, galloping on
out of the great oblivion,
galloping till the night is gone,
he rides upon the wind tonight,
he rides upon the wind.

The headless horseman rides tonight,
he rides the wind alone.
Beneath his arm he tightly tucks
his head of gleaming bone.
His voice is harsh and hollow,
it is horrible to hear.
The headless horseman rides tonight
to fill the earth with fear.

And he rides upon the wind tonight,
he rides upon the wind,
galloping, galloping, galloping on
out of the great oblivion,
galloping till the night is gone,
he rides upon the wind tonight,
he rides upon the wind.

The headless horseman rides tonight
upon his fateful trip.
With silvery scythe of steely death
held fast in bony grip,
he sweeps it swiftly forth and back
as over the earth he glides.
And none in the world is safe tonight
for the headless horseman rides.

And he rides upon the wind tonight,
he rides upon the wind,
galloping, galloping, galloping on
out of the great oblivion,
galloping till the night is gone,
he rides upon the wind tonight,
he rides upon the wind.

JACK PRELUTSKY's verses make his imaginary
animals, outlandish people and horrifying monsters
come alive—RIGHT IN YOUR OWN ROOM! Among his
inspired creations are *The Snopp on the Sidewalk, The
Queen of Eene,* and *Nightmares,* all ALA
Notable Books.

ARNOLD LOBEL's exceptional illustrations for
his own and other authors' books have won
him universal acclaim. His *Frog and Toad Are Friends*
was a Caldecott Honor Book. *Gregory Griggs* and
Nightmares, which he illustrated, and *A Treeful of Pigs,*
which he wrote, are all ALA Notable Books.